Ladybug Ladybug

Edited by Linda Meyer

Paperback ISBN: 978-1-943241-02-6
EPUB ISBN: 978-1-943241-07-1
Mobipocket ISBN: 978-1-943241-22-4
ePDF ISBN: 978-1-943241-27-9

Library of Congress Control Number: 2015943298

Phonic Monic Books
www.phonicmonic.com

C&C Joint Printing Co. (Guangdong) Ltd.
Chunhu Industrial Eatate, Pinghu
Long Gang, Shenzhen, PRC 518111
www.candcprinting.com

First Edition – April 2016

Image Credits:
Cover pg. Kletr/Shutterstock. Editor pg. Kletr/Shutterstock, Dedication pg. Kletr/Shutterstock,http://commons.wikimedia.org/wiki/File:Ladybird_eggs_(7329118990).jpg- licensed under the Creative Commons Attribution-Share Alike 2.0 Generic license; 1, http://commons.wikimedia.org/wiki/File:Ladybirds_hatching_(8284518921).jpg - licensed under the Creative Commons Attribution-Share Alike 2.0 Generic license; 2, macroart/Thinkstockphotos; 3, http://commons.wikimedia.org/wiki/File:Ladybird_May_2008-1.jpg - licensed under the Creative Commons Attribution-Share Alike 2.0 Generic license; 4, http://commons.wikimedia.org/wiki/File:Sa_lady-beetle-larva.jpg - licensed under the Creative Commons Attribution-Share Alike 2.0 Generic license; 5, Asher Lwin/Shutterstock; 6, kurt_G/Shutterstock; 7, Henrik Larsson/Thinkstockphotos; 8, AC Rider/Shutterstock; 9, D. Kucharski K. Kucharska/Shutterstock; 10, 77photo/Thinkstockphotos; 11, Yellowj/Shutterstock; 12, irin-k/Shutterstock; 13, irin-k/Shutterstock; 14, Yellowj/Shutterstock; 15, Yellowj/Shutterstock; 16, irin-k/Shutterstock; 17, Vaclav Volrab/Shutterstock; 18, paulista/Shutterstock; 19, John Foxx/Thinkstockphotos; 20, Kletr/Shutterstock; 21, Vaclav Volrab/Shutterstock; 22, Kletr/Shutterstock; 23, Kletr/Shutterstock; 24, noppharat/Shutterstock; 25, mchin/Shutterstock; 26, BlueRingMedia/Shutterstock; 27, Vaclav Volrab/Shutterstock; 29.

This book is dedicated to my husband and children.
You are my inspiration!

Ladybug, ladybug,

Lay eggs in a batch.

Larva, larva,

You can hatch.

Larva, larva,

You're a grub.

Larva, larva,

Baby bug.

Larva, larva,

Grow real rapid.

Larva, larva,

Eat your aphids.

Larva, larva,

No longer a babe.

Larva, larva,

You will pupate.

Pupa, pupa,

Change inside.

Pupa, pupa,

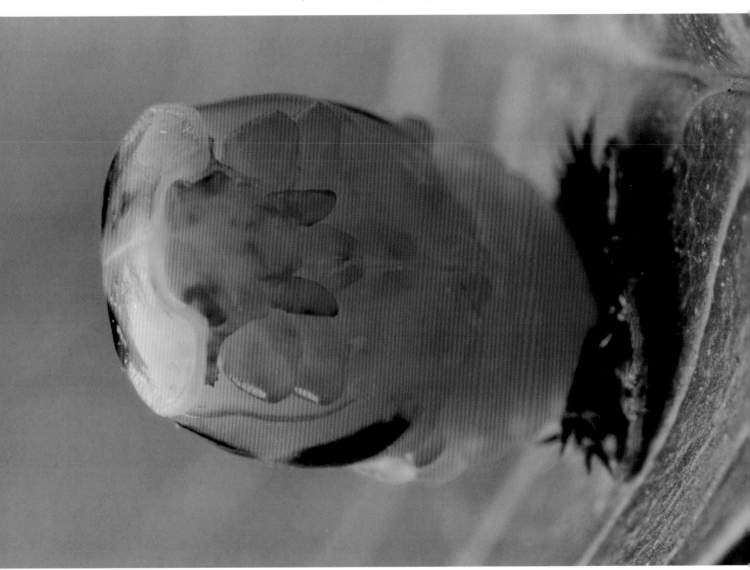

Metamorphosize!

Pupa, pupa,

Come out now!

You're a ladybug!

Wow!

Ladybug, ladybug,

Now, instead.

Ladybug, ladybug,

Dressed in red.

Ladybug, ladybug,

You've got dots.

Ladybug, ladybug,

You've got spots.

Ladybug, ladybug,

You've got style.

Ladybug, ladybug,

Stay for a while.

Ladybug, ladybug,

You won't stay.

Ladybug, ladybug,

Fly away.

Ladybug, ladybug,

Crawl here and there.

Ladybug, ladybug,

Crawl everywhere.

Ladybug, ladybug,

Weather's hotter.

Ladybug, ladybug,

Drink some water.

Ladybug, ladybug,

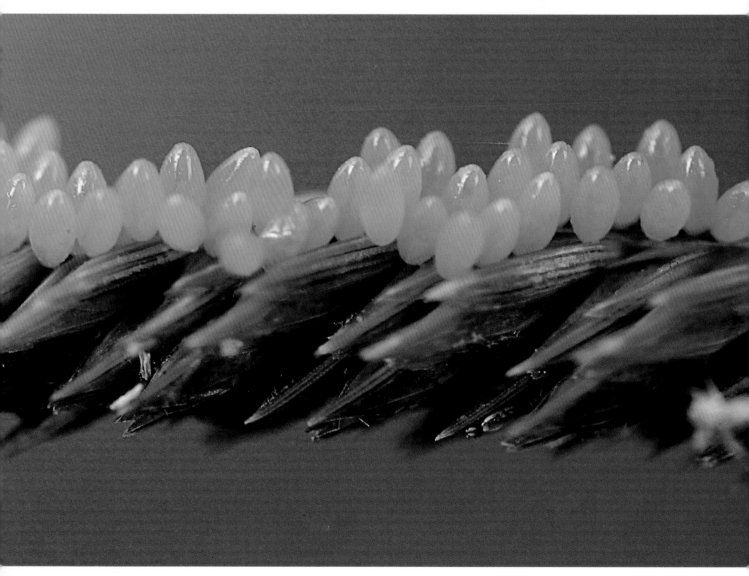

Lay eggs in a batch.

Springtime, springtime,

Eggs will hatch.

Ladybug Life Cycle

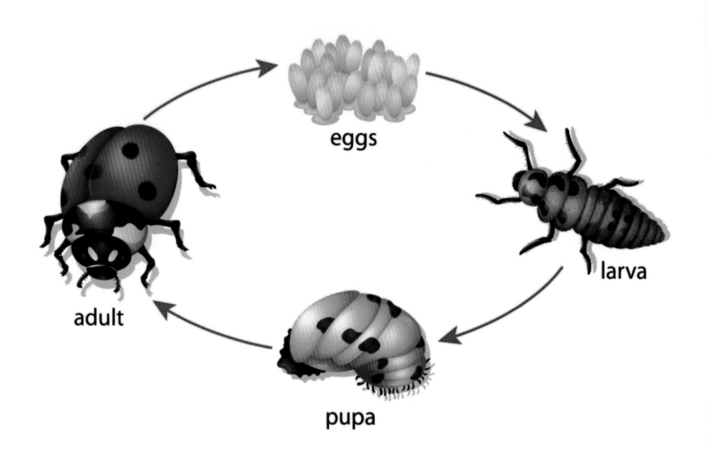

eggs

larva

pupa

adult

About the Author

Cammie Ho lives with her husband and two children in California, where she studied and obtained her Elementary School Teaching Credential and her Master's Degree in Teaching English as a Second Language.

Cammie loves reading books to her children, and is inspired by her favorite children's book authors, Dr. Seuss, and Bill Martin Jr. She is developing an early learning program using music and chants to teach young children, believing that children learn well through a variety of fun channels. She writes lyrics and produces songs that teach reading and spelling in a program called, Phonic Monic.

www.phonicmonic.com